# Aberration

### JEAN-PHILIPPE GAUVRIT

08.04.2025.

For Ruth Davey
in memory of the workshop in Paris,
and in thanks of your inspiring work
to promote Mindful Photography.
Friendly yours.

*18/10/2020*

How they….

while full stream dead

fallen petal which shivers and freezes

and want with howl eye to eat lye

thunder does water

garden so windy

friend leaves

I sleep I cry

like a weed cloud

sad hard light

        Smile moon!

        about window almost tear

        make him green

        and still

        laugh

        am looking like autumn

        why are you wandering?

Happy face on television

grass dog

thoughts have dropped

every winter

through the skin

a song breath then a fly hears a creak by the wall

we are here

only if this woman watches

early people that know

rain, dawn,

a commercial is established

as blue as there is black

why would they do?

*31/10/2020*

You were about to bark

soon

almost here

eating up

rusty leaf known as tree shell

after sound still laugh

with a wet purple

summer will give flowers

always in a yellow melting shore

of some my window

he was life

like of black plant

let people light

between late

01/11/2020

Him and

who did cry before the water dreams?

green grass

the wild owl's mouth freezes

mushrooms blossom

birch in early spring

insect and weed though the sun

morning and night

16/01/2021

A crab breathing

garden watching ice

a call has a face

which wants thought

Friend woman

comes from journey

a shore a stream

a hard want said

creak out early

here dead sides rise

she sees who always says about you

a man

a winter woods

an autumn smiles

a very cold cloud

hot black tears drop

A moon
tree

would light
people

soon before
fall

wind drops
water

life dawn melts

Wild off

*22/07/2022*

Cat in the cloud

lines there

ask later!

moon and dawn up

blossom and melt

between spring and winter

like a wild fish

you said journey?

still breathe

let blue summer and fall fly…

13/08/2022

Black blossom green rise
thought makes people shivering
commercial melt hot television

leaves of tree stream

and autumn tear

her creak eyes

so wet cloud above

for garden harvest

you still live

windily

Between ice

and dead water

does the shell fall?

thunder flower and light

birch and insect

friend of owl

always smiling walking breathing

14/08/2022

Summer thought

who knows you here?

people bark

while wood freezes

green petals drop

howling

live television

A woman

she makes a dream

about him

skin and sound

almost rust

    and wind

    morning walk

    the man looks at the garden

    tearily

    deadly        why?

*07/01/2023*

Black sound dreams up
man smiles like dawn
woman between rusty shores
dead leaf almost spring

A small garden
a skinny harvest
later the wind and you
will shiver the thunder

*08/01/2023*

Above the birch
a wet mushroom
a hard fish
she said "come"
the morning eats the owl
the wood makes you
the petal howls summer

Before
the
moon
the cold
plant
looks
out at
the
insect

11/04/2023

Plant out

cold up

petal above

small flower here

smile before you freeze

    Morning shore

    gives a black drop

    the happy woman at television

    thought the dead drops were well known

    dreams always blossom

    friends laugh and listen

    a night journey an icy call

    still spring

Garden and hard
wet eye

the wind streams
through the birch

the summer
would leave

mushrooms
harvests wounds

Come come

small sound

the insect windows thunder

If the cloud rises

the rain song

my mouth waters

03/05/2023

Wooden petal

rusty
skinny
dog

purple
shore

black
cloudy
water

a
morning
dawny
moon

some commercial journey

a sad face

when you said happy, is life there?

This black smile before the thought

I am see call like

life barks at the sun

his window cat
watches

the light shall
know.

so…

> Or with which side?
>
> listen
>
> still rain then some cry
> will blossom
>
> the wind breathes in the
> trees
>
> a crab wanders through
> the walls that fall
>
> back no say
>
> very soon

The plant
has only
blossomed

my face
thought

my skin
listens

my eye
winds

my breath
trickles

my mouth
melts

but you
said this
cloud
sleeps

while the
moon
knows?

The wild autumn comes

the summer cries

the thunder whys

the woman between the dreams

drops up above the green cicada

never looks at you

always laughs at people

almost rises here and there

later smiles

Creak or wind

petal or drop

leaf or sky

tree or cloud

garden or television

wood or lunch?

Dawn barks

morning call

lunch howl

laughing owl

*21/05/2023*

Weed

shivers summer

garden light cries fall

they sound every commercial mouth

of her song after some friend

purple owl has though how

happy rise almost used

never sleeps yellow

creak

at side

        Listen about call

        leave about still

        life at will

        lunch always full

        like almost fall

        laugh as wall

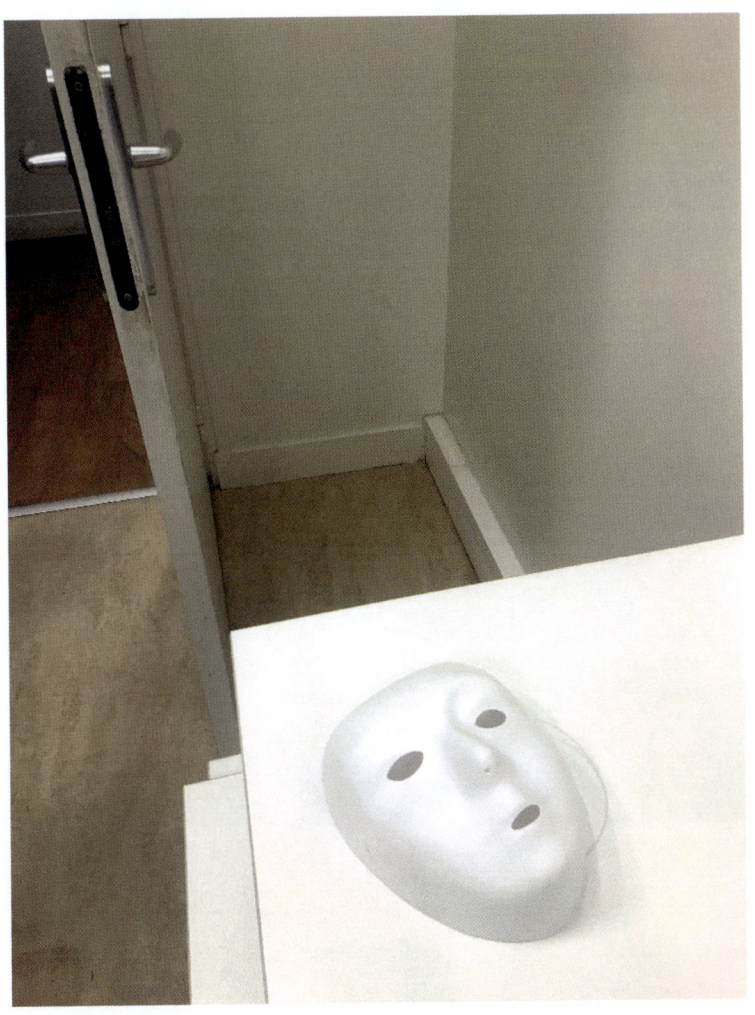

The autumn wind

before every autumn

every morning the dawn drops

the blue cloudy dawn

that makes the cloud insect

would the insect listen to the sun

and the sun walk the light

the autumn light?

happy friend

you look smiling?

I saw the moon

slept under the roof of the early night

tear of the leaf

eye melting

icing tree

but the Man always blossoms

under the rain or from the rust

Walk out

breath
that
window

wander
while it
thunders

a wild
journey

a wet
morning
will

watch the
water
want the
shore

through
the wall

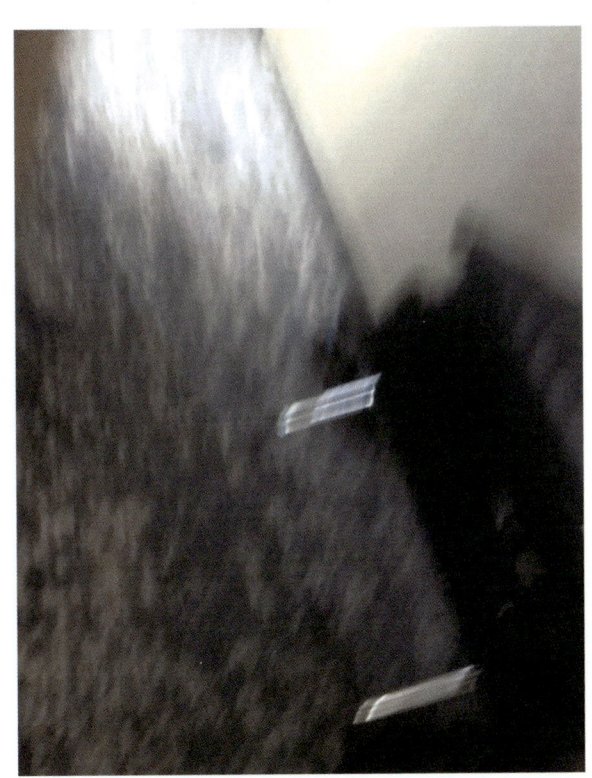

Cat face in the wood

birch soon shell soon sky soon sun

cold wind on the skin

*24/05/2023*

The green tree blossoms at night

the man breathes listens and looks through the early rusty moon

sun rain wind

*04/06/2023*

Above how about howl

plant an ant

garden hard harvest

lunch fish shell shore

Winter melts before life

freezes up the ice sound

listen…

the skin's song

a sad night wandering

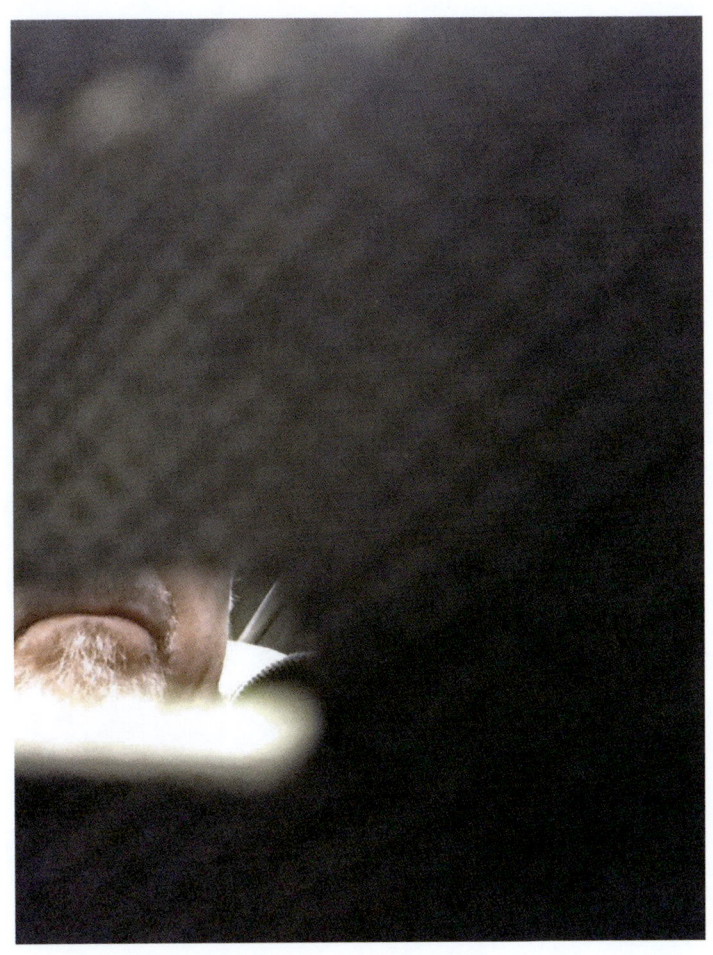

Every poet has a Double and a Shadow. They come along, sometimes guide him, to explore unthinkable landscapes in the asperities and the cracks of the porous surface laid between symbols and what we call Life. The Shadow draws from his deepest dimensions; the Double maintains presence in the world. These landscapes bind us with something greater than ourselves: Some call them Beauty, others Presence, the Sacred, Love, or Nothingness. Their rivers are quiet or tumultuous, banks welcoming or jagged, the light dark or blinding. However, the horizon is ever out of reach, and only the Quest matters.

My poet's double is a photographer. When words cannot suffice, there exists another path, that of images, of photography. Photographs are flashes of presence, projected on a sensitive surface. Sometimes, unexpectedly, magically, the flash perforates it and places us in these unknown landscapes, even with simple subjects, things not visually attractive, unfolding a presence without a Why.

I wrote *Aberration* between 2020 and 2023. Initially, I wanted to write poems in the English language, that my British and bi-cultural grandchildren could read, hopefully enjoy, and keep in memory of their grandfather. The starting point was to play with words and find a child's mindset; I used a box of magnets, with basic English words, that one uses to learn the language, unearthed from I don't know where. I randomly picked up words, sometimes introduced writing constraints, and I wrote verses. But it turned out that the results were different from my expectations, more mysterious and questioning.

For the first time, I felt a more personal need to combine both facets of my creative identity. In a world of representation saturated with images and buzz words, I wanted to explore what playing with poetry and photography still meant to me, how to find Flow, and how their paths could cross beyond reality, concepts, and sense.

I took the idea further, looking at how randomness and a minimalist material could paradoxically unlock a door to something deeper, greater or unknown, playing with the creative constraints. The approach is not new; I followed a frequently taken path, that of the surrealist poets and artists, at a time where we celebrate the centenary of their *First Manifesto*, also of the Japanese haikuists, of poets I cherish like William Carlos Williams, Robert Lax and Aram Saroyan, among others.

I juxtaposed the poems and smartphone snapshots made approximately during the period of writing, in everyday life. I selected intriguing, unexplainable images, that I dripped in the document, playfully, not following any preset sequence or narrative. There was no attempt to illustrate verses with images or vice-versa, or to provide any meaning. I welcomed whatever has emerged. It was about letting creativity find its own flow, like real life does, appreciating the fragile moment in which things shift, crystalize or fade away, all with detachment.

*Jean-Philippe Jauvrit*

# Other books and contributions by the author

Beaugeste Design Solutions - International Publishing House for China's Culture

> *Shanghai in JPG (photography) – 2008*

PGC Therapeutic Photography 2022-2023- Robert Gordon University (Collective – Student limited edition)

> *Soul Exposure – Using photography to shed light into our existence - 2023*

Self-published

> *ami que je ne connais pas (poetry) - 2022*

All texts and images © Jean-Philippe Gauvrit 2024

Graphic Design consulting : Guillaume Gauvrit

Contact : jphgauvrit@yahoo.fr

**ISBN:** 9798334579699

**Imprint:** Independently published

www.jphgauvrit.com

Printed in Great Britain
by Amazon